MASTER COACH SYSTEM: THE COACHING AGREEMENT

DR. LIZ ZED & SABRINA BRAHAM, M.A.

Vividly Visioning Publishing

Tofino, British Columbia

Copyright © 2016 Liz Zed, Ph.D., Sabrina Braham, M.A.

Front Cover Design © 2016 Joe Eckstein

Published by Vividly Visioning Publishing

1182-H Pacific Rim Hwy. P.O.Box 402

Tofino, British Columbia, CANADA

Liz @vividvisioncoaching.com

ISBN: 978-0-9950160-2-6

Legal Disclaimer

This book contains useful information on coaching and the selling of coaching services. This information is presented to the reader "as is" without any guarantees or promises. The authors and distributor specifically disclaim any liability that is incurred from the use and application of the information contained in this book. The authors and distributor make no representations, warranties, or claims whatsoever regarding the accuracy, completeness or legality of the information included in this book. The authors and distributor do not guarantee or imply any earning or benefit due to anything applied from this book.

The authors and distributor will in no way be held liable for damage or loss incurred through the use of this book or any of the information or links included in it. The laws and regulations governing the subjects included in this book vary from country to country and from one jurisdiction to another. It is the sole responsibility of the reader to uphold these laws and regulations as they apply to her own circumstances.

Acknowledgments

In memory of Dr. Byron Eicher, Ph.D. (1934 - 2014), our wonderful friend and colleague. Thank you for lightness of being, your humor, and your life-long dedication to the mastery of psychotherapeutic practice and coaching, and the benefits your wisdom bestowed on us. Thank you for your infinite patience with us as we embarked on this journey together. This series would never have been conceived without you and this book would not exist today, had it not been for your commitment of years to our weekly practice.

How to Use this Book

The way out is through the door.

Why is it that no one will use this method?

~Confucius

This book has its origins in a quest by the authors to explore, deconstruct and describe what it is that constitutes coaching "mastery". The first part of the authors' journey together "began" with a small group of collaborators who were all highly experienced psychotherapists/analysts who were also coaches. At the end of that portion of this journey, the two of us were inspired to write down our experience for the benefit of others who might find themselves on a similar quest. But how to capture everything we had learned in the disciplined weekly practice over the course of four years and 200+ sessions? We realized we could pass on this knowledge more easily through a series of books conceived as bite-sized chunks of information and practice. This written aspect of our project is a book series on the Master Coach System. In each book we will focus on mastering one aspect of a coaching session, beginning here with the coaching agreement. We will reveal what we learned about each topic and how it contributes to mastery based on long-term, dedicated skill-building. If you really want to take years off your learning curve you need to study with people who have already synthesized the very best of ways to learn, and can teach you that. We've put in years of study of our own to master this and we know this way works. Since 2011, we've been teaching our system in group format--and independently mentoring coaches individually--utilizing this system, and the exclusively rave reviews to date confirm that our system works. Here's the secret: change the way you're thinking and that changes the way you play in the world.

To maximize its value we recommend that you read this book through thoughtfully with conscious awareness, at least one time. After you have read through to the end, do the Workout for Results at the end of each chapter. You will need to have at least one audio recorded coaching session, preferably also with a written transcript. Keep a print or digital notebook handy to jot down what you learn about your coaching process. Review the session audio and transcript, making your notes on the practices as they apply to what you find described in these pages. It's a good idea to review as many of your coaching sessions as you have the energy for, and to notice how you're applying what you learn as each new session builds on your skills. The books in this Master Coach System series will provide practical guides to help you hone your craft.

Once you're familiar with chapter contents and concepts, you're in gear and going through the Workout for Results as you review your coaching sessions sequentially, you will be able to skip the chapters, and just apply the exercise questions. Bonus: Are you measuring your progress? If you're really into continuous and never-ending improvement (CANI) and becoming the best you can be in this profession you can use this material again and again and watch your skill and measure how it grows! Not to mention watch your client list expand and your income grow as well.

What You Will Find Here :

- Suggested practices for assessing the content of your coaching sessions.

- Links to downloadable worksheets for making notes about the practices.

- Links to other resources we have created to make the learning easier and to lock in the skills.

- You can earn 24 CEUs for participation in the Master Coach System's six months virtual group practice if you are already an ICF credentialed coach; or 24 BBS (California Board of Behavioral Sciences) CEUs for BBS licensed practitioners.

Table of Contents

About this book

What kind of coach do YOU want to be?

This first book in the Master Coach System® series is for you if you are currently practicing as a life, executive or business coach or if you are an aspiring coach intending to become a more masterful coach. Coaching mastery is not a destination but a journey. What kind of coach do you want to be? If you really want to excel and be the best in your field, we want you to embark on a journey with us that will change you and the way you coach. We are making the core competencies more robust, whether they be the competencies of the International Coach Federation (ICF), or the competencies of any other coaching organization. If you are persistent, want a first or further coaching credential, want to become practiced in the 11 Core Competencies set forth by the ICF, want to transition from a current professional role into a new career as a coach, or you are simply interested in adding coaching to your toolkit, this is a perfect resource for you.

For those of you who are willing to engage deliberate practice to become more masterful as a coach, we share with you some specific practices in these pages. While these first practices focus intently on the coaching agreement, seemingly targeting only one piece of the coaching puzzle, we know from personal experience as coaches and coach mentors, that engaging with these practices has definitively impacted both ours and our mentees' coaching abilities for the better. Our experiences with this material over time have demonstrated consistent results. The coaches we work with become consciously better coaches--more competent, more effective. It's that simple! What more do you need to know? We fully expect that a benefit of studying the Master Coach System and applying the practices set out in these pages will be more satisfied clients who will earn a larger ROI (return on their investment) out of their work with you. We also believe that you will be a happier, more inspired, and knowledgeable coach!

This book though, is not for everyone. If you don't self-define as a lifelong learner, are not ready to commit to the credentialing process, or don't want a guide to steer you through, you're probably not going to be fascinated by what you read here.

The true benefit and satisfaction awaiting you here is the opportunity to reap massive rewards from your expanded knowledge and practice. Get ready to model taking action, strategizing and being accountable. To dive deeper and engage in a learning community with other coaches determined to expand their practice, we invite your application to join our Master Coach System's six month virtual group practice. You can earn 24 CEUs, if you are already an ICF credentialed coach; or 24 BBS (California Board of Behavioral Sciences) CEUs for BBS licensed practitioners.

Please join us on this journey towards coaching mastery.

Dr. Liz Zed and Sabrina Braham, M.A.

Introduction

Inspiration is Always Trying to Get Through

Drifting and floating in the mind's eye now, all the way back to those earlier days as beginner therapists, before we were coaches, to find a rhapsodic reminiscence on why we got into this business in the first place. Everything felt exciting and effortless in those days when we were so inspired by the stunning work of iconic masters. We loved their results. We held them in such high regard. We hoped to recreate the magic with our clients. Their real results had the power of the spell in it, masterful therapeutic work we so humbly tried to emulate.

Today, we have the broader view and the perspective of time. We see the trajectory of time as an evolving spiral, not a flat timeline. On this spiral, we move about from place to place, along and inside it, sliding back and forth in peaks and valleys, with progressive movement forward and sometimes regressions back, and with whole psychotherapeutic "movements" gaining us human ground and losing it.

In an inspiring mid-'70s iteration of coaching, corporate innovation took the form of factory worker input and implementation, and it worked. Interesting to note that 40 years on and counting, we can continue to view this strategic action as novel and innovative! We also know now that clients getting great results isn't automatic! As in the psychotherapeutic process, coaching is as much artistry as it is science.

Sometimes the work can be so very difficult, whether we're talking about our work, our clients' work, or the work of the clients of the coaches we mentor, and it is more the norm that clients struggle regularly with procrastination. Yet, at other times it just seems effortless. We know when we are in a state of inspired action, when we're passionate and enthusiastic, we just roll up our sleeves and get our projects done, or plunge ahead, with no regard to the time. We get into the flow! In fact, time stands still and before we know it the morning's passed; we've forgotten to eat and drink, to grab lunch. We even power through past bedtime and still sometimes, find ourselves bleary-eyed in the middle of the night stoking the fires of creativity, trying to get that last bit down on paper, or down on the canvas. We are trying to capture one last thought, or hoping to wake up just one more day feeling this way--still inspired, still in action!

That idea of staying inspired and in action brought us to the notion of conscious awareness. We were intrigued about how to retain conscious awareness while dancing with the concept of coaching mastery.

As the years passed perhaps we were both lucky--able to retain our passion and the love of our work and our clients. Mid-adventure we sought a greater depth in our work as coaches. We wanted more from the education and credentialing process than was offered. Reignited with a fire to go further, we began exploring with interested curiosity the expansive and limitless reaches of human possibility, imagination, and creativity. We were stoked! We had unbounded energy for this, as we met week after week, for months that turned into years! During this work a motto adopted in grad school became reality: "No efforting! No holding back!" In the inspiration, the doing was effortless.

Pursuing our passion we almost made time stand still and fly, at once.

Standing at the intersection of psychotherapy and coaching, we were seeing with fresh new eyes, passionately driven to learn again. Suddenly now, we found ourselves filled with a thirst to know how far we could go. The word mastery rang in our ears. What did mastery really mean? Was there some "thing" to achieve? If there was this mastery "thing" could we dance with it successfully? What would it *feel* like? How would it *taste*? Or *smell*? What would it *look* like? *Sound* like? We were on a mission for coaching mastery.

We'd like to share our journey toward mastery and where we have arrived today via the elegant system we've designed to guarantee results every coaching session. Today, we'll tell you that there's no actual arrival but a truly awesome experience en route. Coaching is a tool for changing the world. It gives a new lens to transform and change experience. We'd like to invite you along for the ride and to imagine, as we do, the amazing possibilities and opportunities that coaching offers for the planet.

Dream it up your way. We'll tell you at the get-go that you have to park your rucksacks of reductionism at the station before you can embark on the coaching train. And please, for the essentials to bring along: begin with beginner mind. Beginner mind is simple. It is a more open, curious way of approaching things. So remember to notice when you stray away from simple, then bring yourself back to beginner mind. Beginner mind is interested curiosity. It leads to a richer listening. We hope you enjoy the journey through this travelogue of our adventure in coaching mastery. We also hope we can be of service to you afterwards when you decide to board the train and join us, for the benefit of **your** coaching conversations. There you can look forward to dancing in the moment with your client's blossoming magnificence, your joining with their joining, to bring about a richness of living and being--a **lifestyle** first and foremost, yours and theirs. What fun! Please, let's go! Shall we?

Chapter 1 The Coaching Agreement: Foundation of Every Great Coaching Session

And the way to mindfulness, authenticity, and their self-and-other-affirming fruits? Practice.

~Faisal Hoque, Everything Connects

All good coaches focus on potential, affirmations and solutions.

~Sir John Whitmore, author of Coaching for Performance

Do You Want To Be A Great Coach?

Let's look in the mirror of self-reflection. Who is the coach you see there? Who is the coach there who others see? **Who are you** as coach?

So, your clients like you? Maybe some of them love you? Or some, you think, even adore you? You may be inclined to notice their appreciation of your positive qualities. "Sure, I'm a good coach", you say.

Hey, awesome! And guess what? We're being blunt now. Here's the hammer. We hope not to hit too harshly.

Clients **won't keep giving you cash** for your coaching unless one great thing happens…. They have to experience the sticky factor of **awesome results**!

Clients want and need to be successful! That's **why** they seek coaches. Even if your coaching clients like you, and they're also "sticky" (willing to work with you long-term), we're betting that you're wasting a lot of valuable time with unnecessary and unproductive dialog. We believe it's important that you learn how not to do this. There's a lot at stake, both for you personally (clients pay for results) and for the coaching profession in general. Coaching is now one of the fastest growing professions and the reason for this is because it's a major force for positive change in the world. This globally growing coaching profession can be seen as serving up a double whammy! On the one hand, it might mean plentiful potential for acquiring clients and doing something you love. On the other hand, it concurrently means you are swimming in a massive sea swarming with competent competitors. And who are you, if your competitors get better results than you? Do you have a level of expertise and competence and a solid reputation for stellar client results that allows you to stand out? Are you able to market yourself as a key player with pre-eminent positioning? Marketing pre-eminence gets clients in the door. But there is the trap of the revolving door and you could be its victim. Marketing can kickstart momentum while ineffective coaching creates disempowered clients. Don't thrust them back through doorway roundabouts! Whoosh! Can you see them? And hear them pushed full sweep back through the heavy round and revolving door to be dumped out again back on the sidewalk, looking for another coach? They've left you. You're not getting paid!

You've got to be a tremendously impactful coach with fantastic coaching skills to ensure that you can hold onto the fruits of your marketing efforts. How wonderful it is to welcome paying clients and be able to ultimately witness their joy and satisfaction from the bona fide benefits of transformative results on a consistent basis. If this isn't happening for you yet, please do be clear that better coaching skill translates into better client results. The way to embark on the path to owning coaching skill is by first understanding what it takes to become a competent coach. This is not such a difficult task, and when understood, then applied, transforms into skill and artistry consistently and quickly. We will demonstrate here with a first competency how Logical Learning + Practice = Skill + Artistry. Getting the coaching agreement is a foundational competency. Getting this competency down pat will help you weave in the other competencies in a very advanced and elegant way. This is not a one-dimensional practice. It's holographic. Even kaleidoscopic!

In this first book we're going to dive deep into the coaching agreement. Whatever level of skill you already have as a coach, adding an expertly managed ability to establish a coaching agreement is going to incrementally add to client results. We're starting here because the coaching agreement is an essential coach competency. It is the foundation upon which a great coaching session is built. Its attributes when properly understood and deftly managed from session outset, serves quickly to cut through unnecessary and unproductive dialog.

It prevents time wasting. It tames the unruly. Without a good coaching agreement unruliness will arise. Think about it. In those 25, 30, 45, or 60 minute sessions, how much time can you really afford to spend in unproductive dialog, unnecessary utterances and wandering words?

More Productive Time Means Providing Higher Value

Any time spent in unnecessary, wandering, unproductive dialog is time that could be better and more productively used. More productive time with your clients translates to their enjoying a better quality experience, which raises your perceived value. By cutting through wasted time, you just raised your value quotient! That's in one session. Let's make it exponential by looking at the bigger picture. When you stop wasting time with your clients and you create more value, you save time. You can use that time coaching more clients. Time better spent coaching more clients adds more value to the world. Do you agree? More coaching clients manifesting better results in their lives can mean a lot of different things. It might mean more positive attitudes and better functioning in the world of your clients. It might mean the wider world being touched by the outward ripple that your clients create, and almost assuredly it means a greater feel-good impact on your business in general. You become a better coach. You make a bigger impact. Life is better with good coaching.

Before turning a spotlight on what a coaching agreement is and why it's important, let's look at what it isn't. The reason it's important to say what it isn't is because we find a lot of coaches associating the coaching agreement with the coaching contract. Let's be explicit. For our purposes, the coaching agreement doesn't equal the coaching contract. Don't use these two labels interchangeably. Each is necessary. Each fulfills a unique function. You need to understand and employ them differently.

There should be one written coaching contract outlining terms and schedule of service, specifying particulars of coach and client. It's usually put in place before the actual coaching begins. One thing to remember is that a coaching contract may be reviewed and revised any time, as well as from time to time for long-term coaching relationships. When new milestones are created, this would be an example of an opportunity to revisit the contract.

In contrast to the contract, which is structured prior to the actual starting date of the coaching, there is a separate verbal coaching agreement. This is a client-generated agenda for each individual coaching session. It's a refining conversation between client and coach.

- It is intended to reach an agreement about specific, desired client outcomes at the start of each and every session.

- It enables the coach to get information directly from the client about what they want.

- It allows the coach and client to collaborate.

In our Master Coach System, the coaching agreement is a pivotal piece. As an analogy, let's say you're going on a road trip. You've probably heard the road trip analogy used before. We think it's useful here too. Before the road trip, you will probably want to familiarize yourself with the route that will get you from your current location to your destination. People have different favored resources they can use to map out their trip. Think of MapQuest or Google Earth as options, or think of a good old-fashioned folded, paper map. First, pinpoint the start location, then trace it through to a destination.

Once you have your guide of choice, its job is to help ensure:

- You're headed in the direction you intended for your trip.

- You have a successful arrival at a final destination.

- You can locate points of interest along the way.

- If getting off on a tangent, you can seize the opportunity for "recalculating".

We can compare the way that we use a road map for a road trip to the way we use a coaching agreement for a coaching conversation. A coaching agreement serves as key in a coaching session to assist and guide the client successfully to their destination.

A focus on establishing a coaching agreement brings with it shared conscious awareness between coach and client while assisting the client to reach his objective.

- It unfolds consensus on the subject at hand.

- It informs the spotlighting and highlighting of a relevant trajectory.

- Its intention is to create a form or identifiable structure for the session.

Linearity naturally unfolds during the process of establishing the coaching agreement. This precious and important unfolding of linear form may never become manifest at all if we neglect or get sloppy about creating an agreement for the session, or if we are inattentive to it's importance. A focus on establishing the agreement provides opportunity to cut through the meanderings of other-than-conscious contents. These vague and unformulated client contents often take a more wandering, less results-oriented direction and become difficult to rein in and manage efficiently. As a shared conscious awareness begins to be articulated between coach and client the process of creating the coaching agreement begins to unfold with all the subsequent and substantial benefits it holds. A coach's ability to effectively "guide" a coaching conversation is client gold.

Keep in mind--as you begin to work together in a coaching session--that it's not uncommon for clients to have only vague stirrings about where they find themselves in relation to where they want to be, and about what's not right in their world. As you begin to work together, notice where your client lacks clarity about how to proceed. When a client is stuck on a particular "theme of the day" it becomes your job to help your client get unstuck, so that he can articulate something that he can work on. You are a creative thought partner. You don't have to have answers. You don't do the work for your client. You don't know what he needs. You don't have to do these or any other things that presume you to be in the driver's seat! What you do have to do is be able to hold in your mind an overarching view of coaching: what it is; who you are as a coach in this coaching relationship; how to set up each and every single coaching session so that the two of you--coach and client--create a fruitful dialog. What should emerge from that fruitful dialog first and foremost is a client intention for the session. We'll come back to getting the ball rolling on this fruitful dialog and to elicit a client intention for the session in a later section in this chapter.

Most coaches have awareness that their role includes eliciting client statements about what the client would like to get, what she would like to do, be and have. In summary, a key reminder for the purpose of establishing a coaching agreement is that the client doesn't always know. At least, they don't always have clarity to verbalize their intention comprehensibly enough to map out a plan of action. This is key in coaching. One of your coach responsibilities is to help get to this awareness. As the goal is spelled out and clarified, it's important to begin formulating together how your client can get results now, in this session. It should be spelled out in words that speak to getting the ball rolling, in a movement ultimately towards crystal clear clarity. This is a micro part of a macro.

How to Get the Ball Rolling

We've touched on a desire for client clarity regarding an intention for the session via a fruitful dialog. What is the best way to embark on this fruitful dialog? We believe that the best way of embarking has to include acknowledging the critical importance of the coaching agreement. Initially, this means simply taking it on trust, until you've had the opportunity to prove it out time and again. How do you do that? Via experience guiding clients through multiple sessions where they realize results. After a while, it becomes obvious why a coaching agreement is important. No longer wasting time in unproductive dialog is only one of the seemingly many miraculous benefits of deftly managing the coaching agreement. We've mentioned being able to coach more clients, making a bigger contribution, more money. Coach/client collaboration produces better results. That's the ultimate client benefit!

The Coaching Agreement Doesn't Negate the Client as the Expert

We're being repetitious here in the place where we feel that coaches frequently stumble and inevitably get off track. We're belaboring a point that the client often doesn't know consciously what he wants or isn't consciously aware enough to articulate this. While it may seem like a contradiction to the philosophy that the client is the expert, it is not. We need only to dance with these two questions:

1. How do we make the invisible visible?

2. How do we help them have more clarity in their thinking?

At this juncture, it's important to differentiate between conscious awareness and vague notions, ideas and intentions. It's equally important to acknowledge the need for sufficient client conscious clarity to articulate an intention and to map out a plan of action.

Your role as coach is to help your client get to this by collaborating with your client to:

- Get the ball rolling so they can get conscious clarity on their intention.

- Help move them in an active direction toward it.

The Secret to Conscious Clarity and Client Collaboration

The best way to do this is to collaboratively spell out progress. You do this by carving out bite-size, action-step chunks in the direction of a larger goal. Listening to what your client says, you are focusing on the immediacy of this moment and getting results today, here in this session. Whether the outcomes of coaching sessions are ball-rolling beginnings or continuations of work in progress, conscious clarity for the client evolves out of a coach's expert understanding and adept facility for eliciting a coaching agreement.

Reviewing the bullet points of this clarifying and refining conversation between client and coach known as the coaching agreement, remember that it is:

- Intended to reach an agreement about your client's desired, specific outcomes at the beginning of each and every session.

- Allows you to get information directly from your client about intended outcomes.

- Provokes coach and client collaboration.

Superficially, this clarifying and refining conversation between coach and client sounds pretty straightforward. It seems easy enough, at first glance. "What would you like to work on in our session today?" You ask. You hear an answer. Simple! Usually and unfortunately, establishing a coaching agreement is not so simple! There are a host of reasons why not.

The Coaching Session as a 3-Act Structure

How can we make the process of establishing the coaching agreement easier for you? Let's begin by seeing each coaching session as a play with three acts. Act 1 will be the opening act, the beginning; the middle is Act 2; and, the 3rd and closing act will of course be Act 3. A good coach needs to have an awareness of **how to track** the coaching agreement through all 3 acts.

First:

- Did you create a coaching agreement?

Next:

- Are you both in agreement about what it is?

Even so, you will need to be accountable for tracking this agreement once it's established. You must be willing to clarify.

Continuing:

- Are we still on track?

- Is the client getting what the client came for?

We hope you're getting it loud and clear that establishing a good coaching agreement can do a lot for the overall quality of a coaching session. After mentor coaching for a few years now, we're emphatic! One of the main things we're doing while mentoring is reviewing coaching sessions between coaches we mentor and their coaching clients. It is truly such an honor and privilege to witness mentee sessions with their clients. As mentors we strive to communicate this sense of honor and privilege while at the same time communicating opportunities for increasing coach competence and therefore, client results! Mentoring has given us an opportunity to identify some common themes. One commonly appearing theme is a missing, incomplete, or otherwise less-than-adequate coaching agreement. This particular theme of an absent or inexpertly crafted coaching agreement usually highlights and reflects notable moments of needed improvement in so many coaching sessions that we review. In finding such examples in mentee recordings and transcripts we are unearthing valuable teaching moments. As we review the circumstances of these significant contributors to the failure or partial failure of a session, the remedy of applying a well-intentioned and expertly crafted coaching agreement can be viewed as setting a strong foundation for the session. What we will see is how there are signposts to lead us forward and assist in crafting such an agreement.

As we continue to notice and highlight these moments in mentor coaching we can point out an easy remedy through practice. Pay better attention to the coaching agreement! Easier to recognize obviously, once a mentor has pointed it out. For the coach being mentored, it's too late in hindsight, so better chances next time. For coaches unfamiliar with the competency, the old adage "you don't know what you don't know" stands. For coaches who haven't acquired the habit yet, the thought pattern might be "don't fix what isn't broken". Coaches **must be able to trust** that establishing the agreement is purely beneficial. Even before you are clear about how to ensure a good coaching agreement, you must be willing to take it on trust that it's necessary to a great outcome for your client.

When you understand that the coaching agreement is a significant contributor to great client results, you're beginning in the right place. In other words, the right place is leading and proceeding with the conscious intent of establishing a coaching agreement! Now it becomes a matter throughout the session of reflecting back to your client, and tracking whether there's a collaboration toward the same outcome. Are you and your client forming, working toward and getting a substantive coaching agreement? Are the desired outcomes being articulated and jointly understood? In service of this you are providing your client an opportunity for creating an internal reference check. A back-and-forth dialog about the coaching agreement continues. As this is happening, you become more in alignment with assisting your client to reach their objectives.

To further our intention describing the steps in this dance of establishing the coaching agreement, we've created a list of six key components. We call these "The 6 Signposts of the Coaching Agreement" and we'll use this form to map out these key components. We'll devote a chapter each to a more detailed description of each of the 6 signposts.

The 6 Signposts of the Coaching Agreement

#1) Necessary every session

#2) Created in the moment

#3) Client-created vision of an outcome

#4) Coach thinking out of the box

#5) Always the client agenda

#6) Focus to measurable result

Unconscious Incompetence

Are you aware of the obstacles to coaching mastery? Do you know or understand what keeps you from being a really good coach? Whatever you think you want, if you don't have it right now it's because there's ambivalence at work, some other-than-conscious internal dialog that has your self-image telling you the things that you don't want that contradict what you think you do want. So, if you're not getting what you think you want, how does that relate to your intended coaching success? You want to be the best, or the most excellent coach possible and you're either getting feedback from your clients or your mentor, that it's not quite happening. And why is that? We think it's not quite happening because you have obstacles in the way. Some you may know about, and some you don't.

Now, let's consider the case of a psychotherapist or someone else with a history in the helping professions. Let's pretend for a minute that it's you. You think of yourself as being very skilled in your profession. You imagine an easy transition into the realm of coaching clients rather than counseling clients, or another way of working with clients. Perhaps you've been dabbling in the coaching arena for a brief time or immersing yourself in the field more extensively. Regardless of your exposure, you simply don't know or understand right now what you're doing wrong as a coach.

Here's a clue. This is not going to work without updating your perspective. In order for this to work, you have to come at it from a different angle. As an example, being on the lookout for the type of critical feedback that you might expect from more expert coaching colleagues or credentialing evaluators. We are often privy to critiques about coaches being too directive in the coaching conversation. What is this about? What does it mean that the coach is being too directive? A coach may experience this criticism like it's coming at them right out of left field. It can be a hard-hitting, unpleasant surprise and even a shock. Sitting on the other side of the fence today as mentors, we're accustomed to hearing frustrated protests from esteemed colleagues. Here's how these might go: "How is it possible to make a living if we can't be directive?" "How am I going to help my clients?" "I'm paid well for my guidance, expertise and direction!" Typically, as one example, these are colleagues who may be in the process of applying for an ICF credential. Do you recognize yourself in this criticism? We saw this reflection in our own mirrors during our earlier years, making the transition from competent coaches to masterful coaches. We cover this in depth in our 6 month mastery program. The best way to put this criticism to rest and work through such obstacles is within our mastery program practice as you are guided with real-time examples and real-time success, and the recognition that practicing coaching competencies only makes you a better coach.

So, it may be challenging to make the shift from self as expert. "I have answers to problems." "I know solutions that may be helpful." "My experience helps cut through the resistance quickly and efficiently."

A coach with a more client-empowering attitude is one who approaches from the new angle, from a moderately different perspective. "Clients have all the answers they need inside of themselves." If I'm directive with you, I'm doing the thinking for you and you're not learning how to think. This deeply impacts you and your confidence, or lack therof. When I'm holding back on being directive, I'm eliciting your ability to think for yourself. I'm there to hold the space as you think things out. Bob Proctor speaks about this while addressing the concept of the 6 intellectual faculties. "Everybody thinks", we are prone to say. But this presumption is put to question as he asks, "Does everybody think? Is that true?" and counters with, "I think most people don't think at all." What is the meaning of this?

We're programmed to think a certain way. Our behavioral programming, the thought-process is convoluted. This is way beyond traditional therapy. We are now helping people to be empowered. By learning how to think, by accessing their own resources, by grappling with things and coming up with their own answers coaching clients typically expand their potential and thus their world. The term is overused and not necessarily exact but being a thought partner serves as a finer descriptive for coaching in the non-directive manner, or being a vessel that helps people with their thinking. We're questioning here. We're examining assumptions that people think. Those assumptions about thinking humans may or may not be true. It's actually very exciting when we put coaching in the perspective of it being about people learning to think, when we're questioning assumptions. If I'm directive with you, then it's probably not happening. You are not learning to think and decide what is real for you. There are coaches that are directive, but we're talking about helping people to emerge into a brand new paradigm of confidence, and ability to think, and being empowered, and opening up to a potential that will never happen with directive coaching. Masterful coaching is helping to develop humans into a more empowered type of being. There's something very different about the outcome from working with a masterful coach than outcomes from working with a directive coach, but it's also more compelling. You're really helping shift the way human beings function in the world. It has huge spiritual implications as well.

The demand for what seems on the surface to be an initially more challenging client-empowered approach may provoke thoughts and feelings of being adrift. It can feel like "I don't know what to do". The habituated mind reacts and objects! Where are the options? What about time-honored practices and techniques? What about all that past training in various healing techniques? Where do these fit into this new quest to acquire coaching competencies, in becoming adept at establishing, or even understanding such competencies as getting a coaching agreement? What options are available that are allowable now?

Moving Into Conscious Incompetence and Beyond

As coaches we need to get beyond a sense that there are no good options. When we feel this, we have moved past unconscious incompetence and into a stage more like conscious incompetence. We know what we don't know, whereas in times past we didn't even know what we didn't know! Now that we know what we don't know, we grow through experience. With opportunities for practice, we will move forward and acquire conscious competence. And when we have arrived at more skillful practice? Ultimately, after a long, dedicated commitment to practice with real clients, experiencing real results that we have begun to understand flow naturally from the unconscious competence of a masterful coach, we will be wondering how we ever found this daunting!

Sabrina shares a good analogy of such a situation from a frightening experience she once had while on vacation:

In Sabrina's words,

"Years ago I was snorkeling in Hawaii and I was not a good swimmer. We were in Maui. I had heard the stories and warnings that being scratched by coral was a really bad thing. I was moving about, holding onto a kickboard, excited about the brightly colored fish and not noticing the coral. Suddenly an approximately 30 ft. diameter coral appeared a couple of inches below me. I can't move my feet or do anything without getting scraped. I'm trying to figure out what to do but I don't know what to do. I'm not able to move without scraping myself. At first I thought that the man I'm with--who's a lifeguard--is going to come and rescue me, and he doesn't come. And then I see a shadow which is my reflection and I see myself very little. I notice the current moving fairly quickly but I'm not. I take a deep breath, relax and float right off the coral."

Sabrina's analogy from her experience expresses for her the elegance of the new model and its attendant improved results. She says, "I took a deep breath and floated off the coral and it changed my perspective".

We want you to understand that this place of not knowing is not a solid wall--it's permeable. Once you become aware of that, you can learn to relax. Relaxing and noticing shifts into a place of allowing. In that allowing, options begin to open up.

We're beginning here with the coaching agreement. We'll be diving deep with other coaching competencies in the future. First and foremost, we want you to know that utilizing this way of coaching means to expect shift and flow throughout your coaching sessions, as you notice when you are--and are not--in alignment with your client. When you and your client experience presence together the coaching is easy, it flows. You don't need to be an expert. You're in sync with your partner and there's not a lot of efforting.

We're saying that when you get stuck on something it's helpful to move away from that specific thing where you get stuck. Back away if you're noticing that it's difficult or you notice efforting. You may need to take a deep breath and a moment to let silence fill the space between you. The coaching agreement is an aspect of your session that won't be coaxed into being with force or effort. You might ask your client "Is what we're talking about now helpful to you, for the goal that you're wanting?"

It is Not Your Job to Have the Answer!

Similarly, as a coach you don't have to have the answer. In your eagerness to find an answer you will miss deep listening. Your clients are the magnificent owners of their own answers. Learn how to wait and listen, how to go deeper with provocative questions that assist your clients to explore their own needs, wants and resources. Now you are allowing magnificence to emerge and trusting their answers to appear. As you listen, you may notice that what the client says is quite brilliant and wonderful.

Let's move forward and look at each of the 6 Signposts of the coaching agreement. Read on. We offer some practices to assist you in acquiring this important coaching competency.

Chapter 2   Signpost #1 Necessary Every Session

You can't improve anything if you can't define it.

~Max Guinn, Deere & Co.

If I had nine hours to chop down a tree, I'd spend the first six sharpening my ax.

~Abraham Lincoln

Our attitudes control our lives. Attitudes are a secret power working twenty-four hours a day, for good or bad. It is of paramount importance that we know how to harness and control this great force.

~Tom Blandi, 1907 French literary theorist

Getting to the Coaching Agreement as a Disciplined Practice

This use of a coaching agreement is a discipline. It has multiple components, with multiple ways of speaking about what it is. One of its characteristics is that it's usually introduced into the coaching conversation immediately after any ethics preamble. The very next step is to have the client inquire into the question, "What do I want?"

True or False:

It's OK not to have a coaching agenda if the client expresses resistance to it?

What's your intuitive and immediate response?

If your intuitive response is that it's okay to not have a coaching agreement if the client expresses resistance to it, you might want to pause and reflect. You may unwittingly be obstructing your course with roadblocks. You may have already begun veering in the direction of a less than optimal session outcome. You may be facilitating off-track diversions. You may be heading down blind alleyways. You may even be careening completely off-course! At the very least, consider that without a coaching agreement you're slowing down the journey.

This and subsequent chapters will have exercises that assume you will be utilizing recordings &/or transcripts of real sessions with real clients to monitor progress in your journey of coaching mastery, focusing specifically here on the coaching agreement. From here on, we'll replace the words "your client" with "Sam", i.e., Samuel or Samantha to represent a client with a name that is not gender-specific. We're doing this for readability and expediency.

Detours and Derailment Be Gone! Be At Ease, Set Firm Boundaries and

Don't Wander Off

For the time being, please take it on faith that by setting aside the intention for establishing a coaching agreement, you could easily end up taking a detour. Watch out for unintended consequences. Your session may not work out so well. Your client "Sam" may not get hoped for results. Wouldn't it be nice to get paid and have Sam return for another coaching appointment?

Rather than wandering off in unproductive directions why not try being completely at ease, or at least imagining being at ease about setting firm boundaries with Sam? We'll be addressing the question of setting client boundaries elsewhere in this series, but for right now, we want to focus on retaining the importance of establishing a coaching agreement. Remember that resisting creating a coaching agreement--either on the coach's part, or on the part of the client--will be a huge factor in not establishing one. Without a coaching agreement, Sam won't get the same results because the strong foundation of the coaching session is undermined, and a foundation being undermined potentially leads to detour and derailment. When you are completely at ease with firm boundaries, resistance is reduced, and obstructions to establishing a coaching agreement and to achieving Sam's objectives are minimized. By retaining the guiding map and strong foundation of a solid coaching agreement, you are exponentially increasing the likelihood of substantial and truly self-empowering results for Sam. How great is **that**?

There is an additional caution relevant to establishing the coaching agreement. Bracket your own opinionated perspective and reactions! A good researcher knows that while researcher bias is never eliminated completely, it's important to be mindful. Good studies require controlling and minimizing preconceived notions that can get in the way of analyzing participant data and results. Smart qualitative researchers have been taught to notice and set aside, aka "bracket" their own self-limiting interference.

Subjective interpretations easily get in the way of rich individual descriptions and participant results. Similarly, if you will bracket your own imposed meanings, interpretations and assumptions of clients' experiences, you can become conscious of not imposing a preconceived perception of what **you think** clients want, or imposing personal interpretations of what they're telling you they want. To the extent that you are also able to set aside client descriptions of what you hear, as they think out loud about what they want out there in their future, you are bracketing a big picture for them so that you can place attention and focus on the journey the two of you are sharing in the limited time-frame of this one session. Bracketing is a way to get past meaning imported by the coach. Again, we dive deeper into this practice of "bracketing" as a means to circumventing the roadblock of coach-imposed meaning in our mastery program.

To the largest extent possible, put aside your own perception of what you think Sam wants. Meanwhile, bring the focus from Sam's big-picture goal into a bite-sized chunk that can be worked on in the limited time-frame of this one session. Bring a sharp-pointed focus on producing action-oriented results right now. Rather than being concerned now with Sam's larger objective, set that into the context that it will either unfold naturally as a product of being broken down into bite-sized actionable chunks and/or will be brought forward into future sessions. Instead of concerning yourself with a future big-picture objective, hone in on a concrete focus of how the two of you are collaborating in this session. Focusing on a here-and-now collaboration, you make room and flexibility for Sam to think through what actions for improvement can be taken now, so you can join with him and collaboratively acknowledge and conceptualize larger possibilities emerging at a future point in time.

This co-creative process of opening and richness helps clear a client-story haze that may be drifting in front of the two of you. Quite often, a client-story is obfuscating and simply emerges out of an emphatic need for an external source to provide a solution to the perceived problem. It's a pattern of habit that will trap both of you without your gentle but vigilant attention. Once a coach firmly trusts in the resource of a co-created coaching agreement, the veil of external authority can be pulled aside. Simultaneously, the part of Sam that is aware of what is wanted is given room to spontaneously emerge.

Providing Solutions Pre-empts Client Brilliance

Now let's consider the unfolding of a non-verbal communication between the two of you as Sam theoretically entertains a very practical perspective about your role here as a coach. In this scenario, Sam is internally wondering, "What is happening here with this person who I've just paid to help me?" "How is this helping?" "When does a solution emerge?" To which your internal reply is "My role is not to tell you the answer to what you're going to do. No, my role is to give you 60 or perhaps, 25 or 30 minutes of my time, and in that time one of the things you're going to get--among other things to do with authentic presence and guidance--is a clear coaching agreement". This type of unhesitating response about the essential nature and definitive benefit of having a coaching agreement allows something great to happen. It pushes all the distractions and other extraneous stuff out of the way, enabling you together to get to the heart of the matter.

If Sam's brought a story peopled with self-limiting beliefs, it might start off as internal background chatter and sound something like this, "Hey I've got this person--this expert--with me, for this chunk of time, and how will I know if I got what I came for? How will I know?" Once that internal dialog is started, once the meaning of the coaching conversation is brought down to this basic level of interaction between client and coach, then together the two of you can actually craft an agenda that has client heart and meaning. Being familiar with the interactive process just described is helpful, so you can focus on goal-oriented or actionable strategy, because you understand that client results are dependent on these. Sam will be able to describe through some measurement that she got what she came for. She can become a participant-observer in her own movie.

This Is Never a Robotic Practice

Bear in mind, there's nothing robotic or rote about the discipline of establishing a coaching agreement every session, except to intend and act on that very thing. Make sure you and Sam have an agreement on the outcome that Sam, ***your client*** wants for each and every coaching session. As you begin to develop your distinctive style of coaching, consider why it would be helpful for Sam to define clearly what it is she wants to accomplish in your time together in this session. And remember, there are as many ways to go about getting to the coaching agreement as there are individual styles among coaches and individual sessions. As previously mentioned, while the agreement becomes a routine, it should not ever be crafted robotically. The next signpost speaks directly to this point.

Workout for Results
Practice #1 for Signpost #1: Necessary every session

Make use of a recorded coaching session to review each of the 6 signposts as indicators of effectively establishing a coaching agreement. Consider creating a document of notes on these practices, so that you can refer back to them for future sessions with the same client or for sessions with different clients. To assist you with these "Workout Practices" we have created digital worksheets for your record-keeping convenience. You can download these here.

Questions for Signpost #1:

Did you create a coaching agreement that specifies what the client wants to have happen **during the predefined time-frame of this coaching session**?

As you review the recording:

- Listen for any resistance to creating the agreement that might have been expressed by the client.

- After the fact, ask yourself again, "In what way was it helpful for the client to define clearly what outcome was desired for our session together?"

- If you didn't get an agreement, think about what might have been different about the session had you been able to effectively establish a coaching agreement for this session?

- How might you have done that?

Chapter 3 Signpost #2, Created in the Moment

It is impossible for a man to learn what he thinks he already knows.

~Epictetus

I suppose it is tempting, if the only tool you have is a hammer, to treat everything as if it were a nail.

~Abraham Maslow, The Psychology of Science: A Reconnaissance

Simply Speaking....

As mentioned earlier, if we break it down to its most simplistic and basic core the coaching agreement might be an answer to this essential question: "What do you expect to get from the session today?" For now, let's consider this as the first prong of a simple two-pronged question. We'll get to the second prong as we take note of the other signposts en route to the coaching agreement.

What does Sam expect to get today? You ask. You get a reply. Are you fully present and mindfully listening? For this key ingredient, being clear that in the moment describes what you're co-creating, you have to be keenly aware of your own state of listening. Do you even know what it means to listen? It's a life-long practice! For now, hear this imperative: creating the agreement is reliant on good listening. When you are fully present and mindfully listening you are in the moment. Being in the moment you create an opportunity for playfulness. As you demonstrate your willingness to dance in the moment with Sam you invite expansion from the start of the session and throughout to session close.

For now, here are some questions to help you gauge your level of listening:

- Are you so present that you are moving with Sam's energy?

- Are you very absorbed in the act of listening?

- Are you vigilant to the subtler nuances of what the client is saying?

- Are you bracketing your own thoughts about what needs to happen?

We will return to these last questions in later discussions on the topic of listening in our Master Coach System series. For now, let's work from one bare-bones example of the essential "Coaching Agreement" question:

- "What do you expect to get from the session today?"

Think about how you might powerfully craft your own version of this question so that your question will inspire Sam to respond in a three-fold way that demonstrates:

1. A present-centered focus*

2. A topic of relevance

3. Oriented to results

* See Dancing in the Moment for a fuller description of what we mean by having a present-centered focus.

Initially, it's unusual to get a neat response with respect to each of these 3 items; however it's a good practice holding the intention for these as you craft your question in each session. Setting this intention and with practice, it will be easier and freer flowing in future sessions to craft a coaching agreement that's created in the moment.

Assist Sam to formulate with clarity a desired outcome for the session. Try on different phrasing as you spontaneously introduce the topic of the coaching agreement into the session. Think of it as the scenic route to developing your distinctive style of client-coach thought-partnering.

Workout for Results

Practice #1 for Signpost #2: Created in the Moment

Consider this question:

Q: What do you want to work on?

A: Think about an answer that appears to you Right Now!

BEFORE you read any further down the page write down the answer that appeared.

Once you have that answer recorded read the next question to yourself as it is written below.

Q: What do you want to work THROUGH today?

A: Now think about what thoughts you are having that may be slightly different when answering this specifically distinctive question vs. the answer that came to mind as you thought about how to answer the question as it was initially asked.

Again, please write it down.

Notice what's different.

Why?

After you've written your notes, considered what's different and why, you can begin again to move down the page and read the third part of this exercise.

Now, consider another variation on this question.

Q: What BOX do you want to climb out of today?

A: What is happening in your brain as you think about answering THIS question?

Write down what's different.

Do You Know How To Create Client-Coach Rapport?

What is rapport? We're going to talk about what it is at greater length later in this series. But the main idea is you feel a connection with the person and they feel it with you. Notice if there's a feeling of client-coach rapport as you begin to ask for the coaching agreement. If there isn't a sense of rapport, then it's probably time to do an internal check-in and notice what appears through this enquiry. Notice whether or not you understand how it's helpful to Sam to establish a coaching agreement created in the moment. If you don't yet grok the importance of helping Sam define clearly what result is desired out of this session look first at your ability to create rapport with Sam!

As you begin to ask for the coaching agreement, it's essential to be clear on how it's going to be helpful to Sam. Let's assume that you don't have clarity about how this is going to be helpful, or perhaps you don't comprehend that establishing a coaching agreement will increase client results, then we suggest that you go back and read Chapter 1 & 2 again. If that doesn't clarify it for you then we think it is helpful for you to take it on faith before reading on.

Know that it's not important to be perfect out of the starting gate. You're simply continuing to **check progress toward creating** an agreement throughout the session. Both you and your coachee are tracking in parallel as you go forward. The coaching agreement may shift and change. It's fluid. That's the value of making certain that it's being "created in the moment". We're making this "in the moment" point **emphatically** in order to convey to you an understanding of **how this is of value** to Sam.

A coaching agreement created in the moment every session assists to accelerate client potential in 5 areas:

1. Achieving goals

2. Exploring activity at a deeper level

3. Defining arenas of engagement and subjects of focus

4. Greater self-awareness

5. Acceleration of critical thinking

It ends up being about what Sam wants to get from the session, keeping in mind earlier descriptions of what Sam might think he needs, versus a deeper exploration.

Coaches who don't understand the relevance and major import of creating an agreement "in the moment" fail to realize that **explicit terminology related to what's happening now** creates **awareness and impact**. This awareness and impact translates to a clearer understanding of how client ideas and perceptions shift and progress. Simultaneously, it should assist in creating a simpler path to follow-through activity and results.

Quiz:

Mark each of the 20 questions as **True or False** (& decide whether or not you need an answer to #3)

Are We Having Fun Yet? Can you tease apart the good coaching myths from the good coaching practices?

1. It is important to really analyze the problem in detail so that you can come up with the best solution with the client

2. Developing working hypotheses about the cause of the problem will speed up the results for the client.

3. Getting clear on all the obstacles that keep your client from reaching her goals will uncover hidden fears and this is important because.....?

4. The aim of the coach is to make sure the client has solved his problem by the end of the session.

5. It is important to give the client good homework assignments to ensure his continued success.

6. Sharing what has worked for you in your life helps to establish rapport.

7. Complimenting a client for setting a goal that you know will increase her success really reinforces that success.

8. If the topic is very complicated for the client, suggest picking something easier to work on.

9. The more ingenious your question is the better result you will get with the client.

10. If the client does not know what they want to work on, it can be really helpful for the client when you are willing to pick a topic.

11. Be sure and ask the background of the situation so you fully understand what is going on.

12. Your client decides they need to change their diet to feel better. It's a simple problem and you can go straight to the coaching conversation without creating a coaching agreement.

13. Your client describes a distressing recent event so rather than going to a coaching agreement it's more appropriate to express sympathy with your client's plight first.

14. Your client is so upset they don't know how to take action so it's more important to let them vent than to come up with a coaching agreement.

15. Your client has a pressing problem and you have a lot of personal experience dealing with such a problem so there's no need to go to a coaching agreement.

16. You take a lot of time to understand all aspects of the problem so you know the best way to direct your questions.

17. You are carefully making notes on what your client is bringing to the call so prior

to working on establishing the coaching agreement it's more important to clarify that the facts you've noted down are the same as the facts the client is presenting to you.

18. You don't totally understand the subject matter the client is talking about so you can't possibly come up with a good coaching agreement.

19. We should always make the assumption that we don't have the expertise the client has to solve their problems.

20. A time frame doesn't really apply in coaching because there are so many times when you can't really get through the material that the client brings to the session in the allotted time frame. A coaching agreement doesn't really help in these situations.

Look at the link for the Quiz answers 1-20. Go to our contact page to leave questions (w/ email) or to find out more about our Individual & Group Coach Mentoring programs or other books & offers.

Quiz Awareness

- Notice which of these 20 are flags for you?

- What are your habitual patterns?

- What awareness has been created for you here?

- What are the obstacles to being in the moment?

Dangers of an agreement created too soon!

Be alert to the importance of being mindfully present. Clients know and you know how to recognize an emerging, workable coaching agreement. An agreement created too soon can be confining, too limited, or leave you, the client, or both of you without enough room to navigate. There are many reasons for these pitfalls. Such a rich area of investigation as this is worthy of in-depth coverage. This is a brief book of the basics. If our experience serves as a qualifying indicator--in other words getting the basics causes you to be more curious, more excited, even illuminated--we know that with the basics under your belt and the possibilities for greatly amplified coaching abilities just around the corner, you'll be thirsting for more and for going deeper. Then, please apply to join us in our Master Coach System teleconference program.

For the time being, keep in mind that limitations encountered while rushing the agreement could include finding yourself trapped in, or enamored with client story; or, taking a wrong detour that wastes your client's time and money describing vicarious details and embellishments of no consequence. A wrong detour can lead to working through something perceived as a problem or obstacle that isn't. Agreements created too quickly tend to be a product of insufficient, inadequate, or unskillful listening.

Subsequently, the coach may rationalize this inadequacy, or perhaps reframe for the client, while for their part the client may not relate to the coach's reframe.

On the other hand, skillful execution of an agreement is analogous to making it unique and so valuable to coaches and clients alike. What we're doing here is shifting the conversation about the coaching agreement so that its usefulness is better understood. This goes hand-in-hand with perceiving its benefits.

Metaphors in the Moment

Creating an agreement in the moment also calls for consideration of what metaphors will be carried forward. It's a good time for vigilance! If you are bringing your own metaphors into the coaching conversation are you consciously aware of doing so? Do you understand how this could prove detrimental to your client? Do you consider that perhaps you unwittingly and subtly substitute your own metaphors in place of theirs? Clients often introduce valuable metaphors that play a key role in deciphering intention. These can be gold, especially when metaphors are clues to help a coach know what has heart and meaning for the client. Are you tracking these? Notice metaphors arising in the coaching conversation so you can track how they originated and so that when these are coach-suggested metaphors you can be sensitive about whether or not these metaphors are **resonant for the client.** It's so important to remember the significance of not being led astray by either your own or your client's **distractions** of resistance. **Client-suggested** metaphors are a hot clue for avenues that will move us beyond resistance and confusion. We'll have more to say about resistance in future work. For now, know that you will be thrown off with mismatched metaphors and you will be at a disadvantage when you don't get why your metaphors are not as good as those your client provides.

Now let's go back to our Workout for Results:

Workout for Results

Practice #2 for Signpost #2: Created in the Moment

Make use of a recorded coaching session to review each of the 6 signposts as indicators of effectively establishing a coaching agreement. Consider creating a document of notes on these practices, so that you can refer back to them for future sessions with the same client or for sessions with different clients. Again, in case you haven't yet downloaded the Worksheets you can find them at our Worksheet Download link here.

Question for Signpost #2:

Is there a clear demonstration that there is a coaching agreement that has been created in the moment?

As you review the recording listen for **rapport**:

- How was the request for the coaching agreement expressed by you?

- Are there examples of matching the client's energy?

- Was there evidence of effective listening?

- If not, what might you have done differently?

- How might you have said something in a different way to evidence "dancing in the moment" with the client?

- How does rephrasing impact outcomes differently?

Chapter 4 Signpost #3, Client-Created Vision of an Outcome

It takes someone with a vision of the possibilities to attain new levels of experience, someone with the courage to live his dreams.

~Les Brown, motivational speaker

If you don't know where you are going any road will take you there.

~Chinese proverb

You can never solve a problem on the level on which it was created.

~Albert Einstein

Your value as change agent

What value do you bring to your coaching conversations, i.e., why are you getting paid? Have you thought about what makes you a coach in these conversations? As the coaching agreement is a vehicle for client results, how does your intention to use it in service of the best possible outcome for your client--Sam--make a difference? By driving this vehicle forward and steering in the most elegant way, you are in effect asking yourself, "What is going to happen here that makes this session about **coaching**? What is not going to happen here that makes this session not about **counseling**? What is not going to happen here that makes this session not about **consulting**?" You are quietly asking these kinds of questions of yourself so you can stay on course to get the **best results** for Sam.

We have the privilege of mentoring coaches along a spectrum of experience. Sometimes, even coaches who have many years of professional experience, and who may have attained a certain level of expertise in coaching are potentially setting a stage for dire consequences due to not understanding the difference between counseling, consulting and coaching, in spite of all their experience. For instance, imagine you are a coach using the awesome power of visualization and wanting to help Sam--who's seeking a change from habitual, reactive, negatively-patterned behavior--move into a more positive response pattern. Watch out! You might inadvertently lead Sam into an unexpected danger zone by accessing and revivifying a negative experience. The intention may be solid, as you and Sam collaborate with an agenda for powerful results, but when you assist Sam to revivify a negative situation from the past rather than retain the focus on present intention for a new set of positive behaviors in the future, a potential for retraumatization may be powerfully present and therefore harm could result. Sometimes, a coach with a strong psychotherapeutic skill set will engage such an intervention out of habit, out of a non-recognition of the negative aspects of holding a dual role, or out of simply not worrying about consequences because he or she feels skilled to manage outcomes. Regardless of how you choose to utilize your expertise while wearing your coaching hat, it's imperative to be fully cognizant of the potential for harm without a one hundred percent ability to distinguish between--and articulate the distinction between--a coach, counselor and consultant. With the ability to clearly make these distinctions known, you can be more powerfully present to serve appropriately and refer appropriately, while avoiding dual roles or blurred and overlapping roles. It's very powerful work that happens over the course of mentoring sessions, as coaches are becoming keenly aware of and able to articulate those distinctions effortlessly and confidently. We are committed to teaching you a way to do this, so you can have incredible results on a regular basis with your clients, by learning this system. Not everybody's going to want to put in the time and effort, but for those that do, this system is going to help you get those consistent results. Our level of coaching expertise is a scarce commodity and we've worked hard and long perfecting a system of precision and accuracy, and presenting our knowledge in a way that others can really get it.

Again, consider the question, "what is your value as a change agent?" Stay grounded in the awareness that a client-created vision of an outcome is the context or frame around a well-constructed coaching agreement.

Whenever we're growing, we're building new and breaking down old simultaneously. Letting go of what was, takes courage. Creating new mental pathways, takes resilience. To forge ahead in this manner works best in an environment of safety. Thus, the provision of a level of trust and intimacy is necessary in this work we do as coaches. We'll talk more of trust and intimacy later in the series. Would now be a good time to ask if you are present with all your interested curiosity? In other words, are you present in a way that moves Sam to share what's top of mind for Sam? A willingness and an ability to step outside of our comfort zone are often thought of as prerequisites to change. Therefore, as the coach at this party there's an unspoken expectation that you will provide a level of safety to hold client discomfort, as well as a level of provocation to help move client discomfort into actionable strategy. Meanwhile, you're trusting that Sam has the innate ability to move in the direction of these things without you.

It is a big deal and a potentially incredible gift for Sam to have someone truly present who is interested in how she is trying to figure something out. Simultaneously, you are being presented with an opportunity for wonder and excitement, an opportunity to participate in a co-creation of simply allowing the unfolding, and of beginning to move around with it, matching Sam's energy and dancing in the moment.

Some considerations in pursuit of a client-created vision of an outcome:

- Does Sam have something in mind that he needs and wants to work through?

- Are you open to all the possibilities of what that could be? This is a topic we'll return to repeatedly throughout the series!

- Where is Sam's energy? How will you, as coach tap into that?

- What is the desired outcome?

- Does Sam have a vision of what the outcome will be?

- What might want and need to be expressed?

- How will Sam articulate the vision?

In order to maximize the potential of a vision manifesting into real-life concrete experience, it's best to flesh it out in all its sensory splendor:

- Can clients close their eyes and bring to mind a picture of their "vision"?

- Are they able to experience the taste when their vision appears?

- Can they attach their sense of smell to the vision?

- Does it have an aromatic sensory dimension?

- What does the vision feel like as they immerse themselves into its environment?

- How does the world sound inside of a fully fleshed out vision?

- How will clients know when they have their desired outcome?

Workout for Results
Practice #1 for Signpost #3: Client-Created Vision of an Outcome

Make use of a recorded coaching session to review each of the 6 signposts as indicators of effectively establishing a coaching agreement. Consider creating a document of notes on these practices, so that you can refer back to them for future sessions with the same client or for sessions with different clients. For your convenience, if you haven't already done so, please find the WorkOut for Results Worksheets for digital download here.

As you review the recording, listen for the client's **vision**:

- Have you invited your client to express a vision vividly with aliveness, vitality and resonance and is there a sense of collaboration in the response to your invitation?

- Is the client vision specific to an outcome for this particular session? And,

- Is it a true expression of the client's desire, or have you "hijacked" the coaching agenda?

Listen for clues where you might have "stepped over" something the client was trying to address and inadvertently steered the coaching conversation, or appropriated it. For example, did you end up with a coach's script, or **your** version of the client's vision?

Chapter 5 Signpost #4, Thinking Out of the Box

A powerful question alters all thinking and behaving that occurs afterwards.

~Marilee Goldberg, author of The Art of the Question

There is nothing so useless as doing efficiently that which should not be done at all.

~Peter Drucker (1909-2005), American management consultant, author, and educator

Always act to increase the number of choices.

~Heinz von Foerster (1911-2002), Australian-American scientist, pioneer in cybernetics

As a coach you should stay open to thinking outside of the box. Paying careful attention to specific words the client uses is the key to staying flexible, fluid and thinking out of the box. It is your job to piggyback on what's already been expressed and thoughtfully guide in the direction of, and consideration of possibilities.

Playing in the field of limitless potentialities and possibilities produces far more valuable outcomes. Now is an opportune time to assess your ability to truly hold the client as healthy, whole and complete. As a reminder, you may find it useful to continually ask yourself if you are able to hold your client capable of realizing their dreams and visions. And what if your answer is not a solid "yes"? Then we're putting you on notice that it's time to review your passion for coaching!

Ask yourself:

- Can you preserve a space of trust and possibility without making presumptions and judgments and without needing to know "how"?

- Can you hold this space for your client so they can be expansive and express their magnificence without shrinking, without "efforting" and without holding back?

- Can you shine a spotlight to assist your client to find what it is they're searching for? What is it precisely that your client wants to bring to this session and to work through in this session?

- When and if you need to, can you restate and repeat your client's words for clarification and meaning, helping articulate intention and demonstrating you are both describing the same part of the elephant?

- If you are paraphrasing, is your manner peer-to-peer for clarity, vs. parroting with words and phrases that sound condescending, expressionless, or especially too focused on getting it right?

Workout for Results

Practice #1 for Signpost #4: Coach Open to Thinking Out of the Box

Make use of a recorded coaching session to review each of the 6 signposts as indicators of effectively establishing a coaching agreement. Consider creating a document of notes on these practices, so that you can refer back to them for future sessions with the same client or for sessions with different clients. Worksheets on the 6 Signposts of the Coaching Agreement can be downloaded here to conveniently review your individual coaching sessions.

Questions for Signpost #4:

As you review the recording, listen for being **trapped in corners**.

- How was the process of arriving at the coaching agreement expressed?

- Was there a sense that the client felt supported while fleshing out a desired outcome for the session?

- Was your coaching pertinent, reflective and indicative of a safe container while also providing boundaries, in such a way that limitless possibilities might emerge? Were you able to do this without expanding so wide as to invite derailment?

- Are you aware of room to refine and clarify as the session progresses through Acts 2 and 3, demonstrating tracking to stay on course with the coaching agreement?

Chapter 6 Signpost #5, Always the Client Agenda

"A caterpillar, a tiny acorn, an apple blossom all have intention built into them. That caterpillar becomes a butterfly, the acorn a giant oak tree, the apple blossom an apple."

~Dr. Wayne W. Dyer, author, The Seven Secrets of a Joyful Life

Healthy, Whole & Complete

Coaching is ***Always*** about the client agenda. In the coaching relationship the client is healthy, whole and complete. This is relevant to the establishment of the coaching agreement and signpost #5 is a good one because it's a reminder of who Sam is in this coaching relationship.

Coaching In a Timeline of Psychology

Now is a good time to shine a spotlight on some history to really ground and remind ourselves about the importance of holding our clients in this view. Let's consider some of the original roots of coaching as they've grown in the field of psychology. One of those fertile birthing grounds has been humanistic psychology, also known as 3rd force psychology. While it can be clearly demonstrated that cognitive-behavioral psychology is foundational for coaching, both 1st & 2nd force psychology, psychoanalysis and behaviorism respectively, have built their 100+ yrs. of scientific research via studies of pathology and dysfunctional behavior. Meanwhile, the humanistic camp takes the self-actualizing nature of humans as its ground of being. (*Self-actualization is preceded by the fulfillment of survival needs.*) Humanistic psychology's founder Abraham Maslow took for his new psychology's model a view of the individual as healthy, with the innate propensity for self-actualization. Positive psychology is an outgrowth of humanistic psychology and has been wholeheartedly embraced by coaching in recent years. Maslow's model is absolutely aligned with a now-standard coaching view of clients as "healthy, whole and complete". If the ICF is not the premiere responsible party for coining this four-word phrase describing coaching clients, at least the ICF holds this tenet as basic to a coaching mindset, and as a basic tenet it has greatly influenced really good coaching.

Toward A Regulated Profession Of Coaching?

There are distinctive views among various schools of thought relevant today, as different governing bodies and professional associations, organizations and educational institutions in psychology, coaching and other "helping" professions will be pressed to consider the future of coaching in a global community. This is a provocative and controversial topic, and as you work with us we will be tapping into these distinctions, as we explore their relevance to the coaching profession and practice, in future works related to our Master Coach System.

We're All Finding Our Purpose

We like to think of the client as magnificent. Every individual is uniquely formed and combined into a whole such as has never before existed. Each and every client comes complete with their own distinctive features and patterns of behavior, constellated out of an unfathomable ocean of possibilities. All of us are conceived from this ocean of possibilities, and then grow through various stages from this ocean of possibilities, unique and singularly distinct, each from every other. We are privileged to a unique pre-birth environment. Throughout our life cycle we continue to experience a unique interaction of nature and nurture. While we traverse the life journey on an individual path it can also be said that we are each a singular representation of a larger cosmos connected and comprised of seemingly unlimited possibilities. Now we move beyond the confines of humanistic psychology, into the realm of transpersonal psychology and beyond. Coaching as a profession has many roots and will continue to morph and grow. The possibilities are limitless and there's a lot more to come as we forge forward into the future.

As coaches we must keep at the forefront this view of the client as healthy, whole and complete. Our coaching sessions can thrive when focusing on the agenda of the client. Now we'll return to Signpost #5 and how it's relevant to establishing the coaching agreement.

Beware of Dragons, & Carry 2 Keys To The Magic Kingdom Of Coaching

If we follow the 5th signpost it will guide us in the direction of an expertly crafted agreement. Beware, vigilance is required. It is essential to remember to keep a focus on

Sam's agenda, and there are two keys here that we must safeguard to arrive. Remember these two keys.

1. The first key is to have a clear vision of the "coaching landscape".

2. The second key is to know and understand the importance of "getting out of our own way".

Key #1 Getting a Clear Vision of the Coaching Landscape

Stand firmly on solid ground and acknowledge the importance and absolutely essential need of establishing a coaching agreement. Understanding the purpose and intricacies of a coaching agreement encourages practicing with intention to establish one every session. Knowing why you want to have a coaching agreement in place every session assists you to be fully aware in the moment, and matching Sam's energy, especially when you understand two things.

- One of those things is knowing that a coaching agreement needs to be tailored. You should be aware of delivery and how your unique, individual coaching style is pertinent to successfully establishing a coaching agreement at every session.

- You also need to know how establishing the coaching agreement is expansive. You should be clear that it contributes in a most positive way to your coaching client's success.

Key #2 Getting Out of Your Own Way

A focus on your coaching client's success dovetails with key #2. It's important for you as a coach to get out of your own way. What we mean by this is that you set an intention and regularly make a practice of letting go of self-conscious focus on how you are coaching. This can be a double-edged sword. Even as we drop the self-conscious self-critic who damns our coaching ability, we struggle with striving to get all the coaching competencies covered in a single session! This calls for courage and trust. It takes courage to retain single-minded focus on being in service to the client-desired outcomes for the session, and the magnificence of the client you are serving. It requires trust in the importance and relevance of establishing a coaching agreement to contribute positively to that end.

Secrets to Clarifying the Coaching Agreement

It's all too easy to make assumptions about what Sam is saying he wants to accomplish. Very often there is a need en route to establish the exact terms of the agreement while deconstructing Sam's terminology. That way you arrive together at something that is not only "doable" but also in parallel. An aware level of coaching skill requires that you establish that both you and Sam understand similarly what Sam means while describing what is wanted. We need to have an almost insatiable curiosity about clarifying and tracking our client's agenda. We need to be vigilant to any possibility that we may inadvertently insert our own agenda. Always remember, this is about Sam's agenda, not the coach's agenda.

As coaches, we're waiting for clients to take the lead on their own agenda. We're ready to help them comprehend and express with more clarity what that agenda is. As previously mentioned in Chapter 1, we're **helping** them to **become conscious** of what it is that's percolating and **why they wanted to have this session**. We are prepared with one of our most important tools--a potentially relentless curiosity, presented in the form of powerful questions. This is accompanied by a willingness to go deeper, to not stay satisfied with superficial utterances. We want to do all this while at the same time having no vested interest in a particular outcome for Sam.

Now a shift in your coach mindset could be in order. Would it be helpful now to acknowledge that you might not know exactly how to do this? As we've mentioned earlier in Chapter 1, it is **not your job** to have the answer. If you're accustomed to thinking of yourself in more traditional terms, as the one with the answers, you've now got to shift from "I'm the expert so I should have answers", to "through our work together, clients can arrive at their own solutions". For the expert who is you perhaps this is a different pattern of thinking!

Let's consider again a couple of critiques that might arise with respect to coaching competency:

1. A coach is **too directive**. While the point has already been raised, this can actually be a conundrum: you need to know HOW to be directive while being aware of the need NOT to be directive, so you can allow the **client to have absolute choice** in the session agenda.

2. A coach must be completely at ease with setting firm boundaries with their client

because resistance has the potential to be a huge factor in not getting a workable coaching agreement.

During those moments of self-observation when you are able to see yourself as overly directive, think about stopping and asking yourself, "What's the underlying motivation for giving the answers here? Why do I have a tendency to lead my coaching client?" Even though I see there's something Sam doesn't know how to do, at this point I can ask myself how figuring it out for her at any time is actually running a risk of handicapping her. **Beware** of short-circuiting the critical thinking process for Sam. When you have conscious competency intact you are more likely to allow Sam to get to the destination on her own steam.

A coach, therapist, or other helping professional who has all the answers is assisting to keep their clients "stuck". Instead, assist them to tap into their own resourcefulness, to utilize their own critical thinking and to come up with their own solutions. Empower your unique and wonderful clients to tap into all the skills, strengths, talents, abilities and magnificence they have within them.

Workout for Results

Practice #1 for Signpost #5: Always the Client Agenda

Make use of a recorded coaching session to review each of the 6 signposts as indicators of effectively establishing a coaching agreement. Consider creating a document of notes on these practices, so that you can refer back to them for future sessions with the same client or for sessions with different clients. We hope you're finding our 6 Signposts Worksheets super helpful when it comes to tracking your ability to establish a coaching agreement every session.

Questions for Signpost #5:

As you review the recording: Listen for the **agenda of the session**.

- Whose agenda is it? What are the clues? As you attentively review precise words and phrases of your client what do you notice?

- Do you "lose", "side-step" or "step over" any significant client words or phrases?

- Does your client appear to be demonstrating resistance in getting to a coaching agreement?

- In what specific ways are you noticing resistance or avoidance in this session? If so, what's your part in this?

- Do you demonstrate support with questions to stimulate an inner search for a workable agreement?

- Are you taking your cues from your client's direction or are you being overly directive?

- Are you trying to "figure it out" for her?

- Is the client bringing metaphors into the conversation?

- Are you picking up the thread of the client's own metaphors?

- Are you introducing your own metaphors into the conversation? If so, are you noticing whether or not these are resonant for the client? How do you know?*

***Caution:** If you find yourself introducing your own metaphors, listen for client congruence, and also listen for the potential for these to "derail" the conversation and the client.

As you consider these practices for the purpose of crafting an agreement from Sam's agenda, this is a good time to remember the practices from the previous signpost #4 as a coach who stays open to thinking out of the box. We mentioned that you will be paying careful attention to specifics of what your client is saying as you simultaneously stay grounded in flexible and fluid, creative thinking, mindfully guiding in the direction of Sam's possibilities.

Chapter 7 Signpost #6, Focus to a Measurable Result

That which is measured improves.

~Old Business Adage

You can't improve anything if you can't define it.

~Max Guinn, Deere & Co.

There is nothing so useless as doing efficiently that which should not be done at all.

~Peter Drucker

Can it be put in a wheelbarrow?

~Stephen Brooks, clinical hypnotherapist, British Hypnosis Research

Scenario:

Coach asks client, "What do you want to work through in our session together today?"

Client responds, "I'd like to feel better about this whole situation. I'd like to be able to put it behind me."

Coach, "And at the end of our session when our call is complete, how will you know if you have accomplished that?"

Remember when we mentioned a second prong? It was back there at Signpost #2 Created in the Moment. We talked about a basic two-pronged question.

Remember also, that we like to think of each coaching session as a 3-Act play. Each act occupies one of the 3 segments: beginning, middle, and end. We believe the coaching agreement should be tracked through each of the 3 acts. We need to be constantly coming back to an awareness of whether or not we're still on the coaching agreement.

To that end, here are some questions we can ask ourselves: Did we create a coaching agreement? Are we still on track with the same agreement, or has it gone off track? Does it need tweaking? Is the client moving towards getting what they agreed they wanted to accomplish in this coaching session?

If we haven't made an agreement about how Sam will know whether or not she has gotten what she wanted in this session together today, then how will either one of us know? How will the coach know? How will the coachee know?

This is why it's so important to give due care and attention to the 2nd prong of the 2-pronged question we spoke about from the earlier pages of Chapter 3.

1st prong: "What do you want?"

2nd prong: "How will you know?"

It's important to be paying attention to how Sam will know. The key piece here is measurability. There's impact when clients are able to put into words how to meaningfully measure a desired result. You are guiding this exploration. You are assisting Sam to articulate the experience of knowing. How will you accomplish this? What will have to happen for him to know and respond with a resounding "yes"? What question or approach will you bring so that Sam can determine and verbalize what wants to be accomplished today? How will you track this? How will the two of you stay on track? Did Sam get what he wanted from the session? When you have pursued the agreement with clarity and intention Sam will know a solid **"Yes!"**

This most important clarification for how to know if the desired results are achieved in the coaching session needs not to be forgotten! One of our former hypnosis teachers taught us this way to think about the client's description of their desired outcome: "Can it be put in a wheelbarrow?"

As we try to determine whether or not the result is measurable, whether or not clients will know they have the result they came to their coaching session to get, the wheelbarrow metaphor offers a nice way to begin to dance in the vocabulary of the client. As you assist in the teasing out of descriptive words good enough to describe a measurable outcome, the right ones will evoke a tangible sense of "yes" or "no". The answer to "Did you get what you came for?" will evoke a clear and distinguishable "yes" or a clear and distinguishable "no". When you're helping find ways of describing intention so the clear and distinguishable "yes" or "no" is recognizable, this is good guiding and coaching! Tracking measurability through the 3 Acts of a coaching session is even better guiding and coaching. This is the kernel at the heart of an expanding mastery that comes from an effective implementation of a coaching agreement.

Workout for Results
Practice #1 for Signpost #6: Focus to a Measurable Result

Make use of a recorded coaching session to review each of the 6 signposts as indicators of effectively establishing a coaching agreement. Consider creating a document of notes on these practices, so that you can refer back to them for future sessions with the same client, or sessions with different clients. <u>Worksheets for Signposts 1-6 download link here</u>

Questions for Signpost #6:

Measurability magnifies the amount of money you make. As you review the recording, listen for **measurability**:

- Where was the exercise of crafting a measurable result first introduced in the coaching conversation?

- Did you use a "how will you know" question? What specifically did you ask?

- How did you track your measurable for the coaching agreement for this session? How did you manage your client's progress toward that measurable and determine whether or not she is getting it in this session?

- Are you so clear on how your client measured their results that you can describe it to another person? Write it down.

- Did you get a sense that she felt supported as she fleshed out how to measure results?

- Did you honor boundaries by tracking the process of a measurable result without inviting derailment?

- Was there refinement and clarification with timeliness through acts 2 and 3, and a measurable result acknowledged prior to session close?

Chapter 8   In Appreciation of Magnificent YOU!

YRTH *You Rock The House*

~<u>The Free Dictionary</u>

Because You DO Rock the House

Congratulations are in order for being magnificent. As a masterful coach you want to be an example of what you espouse as a coach. Consider how you will reward yourself for having prioritized your time so that you could read this book and do the practices. Now it's time to celebrate!

In recognition of your unique magnificent self, hopefully you intend and follow-through by celebrating in a way that has heart and meaning for you. As refreshing revitalization springs forth out of celebration and an inspired energy reappears, it will be time once again to capitalize on the momentum and ask yourself "what's next"? How will you continue to move forward?

Congratulations on putting all the effort and learning into improving the coaching agreement and noticing what's different about where you were before practice with the agreement and where you are now. You've probably noticed yourself moving in and out of your comfort zone, stretching and growing! As you've been practicing what do you notice about your ability to get a coaching agreement in your client sessions? By allowing yourself the opportunity to become consciously aware of noticeable changes in your coaching session experiences and client results, expanded vistas like concentric circles of possibility can come into view. Depending on whether or not you favor the function of compound interest perhaps you can humor us here & see it as tapping into a power not dissimilar. (Even if the "8th wonder of the world" quote has now been attributed actually to no one & the concept claims overrated.) Truly though, it's hard to argue with the power of masterful coaching! Masterful coaching is indeed a force of change for good in the world. We're not aware of anyone disputing that. Your work as a coach assists other individual humans to tap into their unique magnificent selves and purpose, and make their contribution for a greater good via intention-setting and strategic action-taking. **Now imagine the possibilities!** We'd love to hear from you. Contact us here.

High five for your dedication, perseverance and hopefully your resilience as you continue to cultivate your art and craft of coaching. You are obviously someone who has the desire, commitment and most likely the resiliency of a really good coach. In fact, you are right now pursuing mastery. Sabrina & Liz embrace coaching mastery as a life-long practice and we are passionate about becoming the best coaches and coach mentors that we can be. It is our intention for you to benefit from our practice as we send out ever-expanding outward rippling rings to touch you as you read of our experiences and are supported in practice with our Master Coach System® sessions. We are here to help you be the best coach you can be, with better client results, more clients, more money and a fulfilling expression of your passionate, vital and magnificent self through coaching. As fellow coaches we are appreciative and joyous to share this path with you!

About the Authors

Sabrina Braham, M.A. MFT, PCC, an executive coach since 1978, works with Fortune 1000 companies and is a certified mentor coach leading workshops with Dr. Zed.

Sabrina specializes in mentor coaching for psychotherapists who want to improve their coaching ability. She has an extensive background in corporate work. Her Corporate focus is on C-level executive coaching, consulting, leadership development, and team building for change management and performance improvement. She also coaches on conflict resolution and helps clients increase emotional intelligence for higher profits, productivity and improved morale. Sabrina has a passion, extensive experience and an online radio show that helps women advance their career and leadership skills.

Her clients range from Fortune 1000 companies to individual coaches who want to fine-tune their skills. A partial client list includes: Stanford University, Farmers Insurance, Army Corps of Engineers, State of California, Dominican Republic Tourism and USAID (United States Agency for International Development).

Learn more about Sabrina and her current projects at www.SabrinaBraham.com Access free interviews on leadership and business success at: WomensLeadershipSuccess.com

Liz Zed, Ph.D., MCC, certified executive & business coach is the co-developer (w/ Sabrina Braham) of the Master Coach System® using masterful methods to mentor coaches worldwide.

Dr. Liz Zed, Ph.D., MCC combines her entrepreneurial leadership & clinical supervisory skills into a focused dedication & passion for the advancement of professional coaching. Her global clientele of experienced licensed professionals plus individuals aspiring to their first professional credential generally expand their horizons into coaching because they have a passionate affinity for both the core values of coaching &/or an experienced or intuitive knowing of the power of masterful coaching, fuelling their desire to engage at a deeper level.

Zed & Braham's combined deep listening skills, intellect & decades long immersion in change management techniques has evolved the Master Coach System® which now provides the opportunity for others--quickly and effectively through interactive practice--to bring the power of masterful coaching as a profound skillset to their own clients for massive impact and exceptional results. To have a bigger impact with your coaching, see your clients get better results, & learn how to implement new change technology from someone who knows how, get connected HERE now.